ALL ACTION

CANOEING

ALAN FOX

Wayland

Titles in this series
Backpacking
Canoeing
Climbing
Mountainbiking
Skiing
Street skating
Survival skills
Wind and surf

Series editor: Paul Mason
Editor: Paul Bennett
Designer: Bridgewater/Kudos Editorial and Design Services

Picture acknowledgements: Brian and Cherry Alexander 12; Allsport 7 (top, Cirotteau-Lambolez), 10 (David Cannon), 17 (bottom, G.Planchenault), 39 (Howard Boylan); Eye Ubiquitous 8 (Paul Prestidge), 9 (Thomas), 24 (David Higgs), 35; Alan Fox *back cover*, 6, 7 (bottom), 15, 18, 19, 20, 21, 22, 23 (both), 26, 27, 28, 29, 40, 41, 42, 43, 45; Tony Stone Worldwide 30 (Tony Tickle); Tony Tickle *front cover,* 4, 7 (top), 25, 31, 32, 33, 34, 37, 38; Topham 5, 16 (Leif R. Jansson); ZEFA 11, 36. Artwork on page 13 by Brian Davey.

First published in 1992 by
Wayland (Publishers) Ltd
61 Western Rd, Hove
East Sussex BN3 1JD, England

© Copyright 1992 Wayland (Publishers) Limited

British Library Cataloguing in Publication Data
Fox, Alan
    Canoeing. – (All Action Series)
    I. Title II. Series
    0797.1

HARDBACK ISBN 0 7502-0243-2

PAPERBACK ISBN 0 7502-0521-0

Typeset by Malcolm Walker of Kudos Design
Printed by Rotolito Lombarda, Italy
Bound by A.G.M., France

Contents

INTRODUCTION

There are many different types of canoeing to try. You could be paddling across a lake, enjoying a week-long expedition on a river or experiencing the thrill of white water. Canoeing offered me freedom from school sports and the chance of an adventure. It also gave me confidence, as I found myself doing things I would never have thought possible before.

I learnt to canoe with a youth group I belonged to. The leader was mad keen on canoeing. We learnt the basic skills on the local canal. As my confidence grew I began to try new moves and dared to venture into faster-moving water. Capsizes were common, but I had already learnt to bail out and swim, with my boat, to the shore. A quick empty and I'd be back on the water to try again, wet but still keen.

There were two advantages of learning to canoe with a youth group. It organized weekends away, and everyone was just as bad (at least at the start). Learning with people who are more skilled than you can be depressing, because they can make you feel as though you'll never be as good as them.

RIGHT

Kayak touring on the River Ardeche in France.

LEFT

Kayaking is a good way of making new friends.

It was the weekend trips away that gave me the real taste of adventure. Late on Friday nights, cramped in a rattling old van towing a trailer stacked full of kayaks, we would head north to Wales. We would end up sleeping in the loft of a farmer's barn, and after a breakfast cooked up on wheezing primus stoves we would drive on, to the first river.

When we got there we would all bundle out of the van and peer over the nearest bridge at the river below. Was the water level high or low?

Don Starkell and his son, Dana, completed a 20,000-kilometre canoe voyage. Starting in Winnipeg, USA, their route took them up the Red River, down the Mississippi, round the Gulf of Mexico and the Caribbean, up the Orinoco and down the Negro and Amazon Rivers. Despite encounters with sharks, crocodiles, piranhas, whales and scorpions, the most trouble they had was from other people. During their two-year voyage they had been arrested, shot at, jailed and set upon by pirates.

What would the rapids be like? The enthusiasm was infectious and soon we would be carrying our boats down to the water's edge, togged up with warm clothes, buoyancy aids, spraydecks and helmets. Our hearts would be thumping in anticipation. The tales we had heard of monster rapids eating kayakers whole could all come true in the next few hours.

I vividly remember my first ever rapid and the feeling of fear brought on by the unknown. The waves crashing down on the deck of my kayak threatened to capsize me, but I survived. All the skills I had

ABOVE

Calm waters in the Lava Canyon on the Bio-Bio, Chile's longest river.

learnt on flat water came to my aid, and my fear dissolved into excitement. I was hooked. Canoeing offered a whole new world of adventure, an adventure that I'm still enjoying today.

I had a go at all the different kinds of canoeing. The peaceful silence of calm, secluded rivers. The crashing turbulence of white water. The power of the sea as you paddle out through the surf, and the magnificent scenery of coastal cliffs and caves. The thrill of competition, racing against the clock, alone on wild river descents or avoiding slalom gates whilst the spectators cheer you on. Whatever I was getting into I made new friends and visited new places. Best of all was the enjoyment of messing around in boats.

ABOVE

A kayaker
punching through
the rapids.

RIGHT

Waterfalls can be
part of a river
descent, but they
require caution.

GETTING STARTED

Taking up a new sport on your own can be difficult, so the best way to learn to canoe quickly and safely is to get expert help.

Many towns have a kayak club and many schools and colleges take their students canoeing. Local kayak clubs usually run their own courses from one-day, 'come and try it' sessions to a complete beginners' course that might last a week. The advantage of a course is that you learn with people of a similar ability. It is also more fun to learn with other people. For safety, you should never canoe alone or in a group of less than three people.

Your first lesson will cover the basics of canoeing. You will learn about the equipment, clothing, essential safety precautions and techniques for paddling in a straight line and turning the kayak. Further lessons will build on these skills, as you gain the experience that will lead up to your first day trip.

On most courses all the equipment is provided. All you need to take is suitable clothes. If your course is in the summer months this would be shorts or track-suit trousers, a T-shirt and warm top and a waterproof cagoule. You are almost certain to capsize, so make sure you take warm

LEFT

Kayakers 'rafting-up' as part of an introductory course.

clothes to change into. On your feet you should wear strong trainers.

If the course is in the spring or autumn then a wetsuit should be worn. The type most favoured by canoeists is a long john, a full-length, one-piece wetsuit without sleeves. This lets your arms move freely. Wetsuit boots keep your feet much warmer than a pair of wet trainers. If you will be doing a lot of canoeing you should get a special canoeing cagoule. These are designed with tight-fitting cuffs and collars to stop water getting in. In cold weather a woolly hat stops heat escaping from your head.

Safety tips
● *Always wear a life jacket or buoyancy aid.*
● *Wear a helmet on rocky rivers.*
● *Wear strong footwear and carry spare warm clothes.*
● *Know how to cope with a capsize and rescue.*
● *Fill all spare space in the craft with buoyancy bags.*
● *Never paddle alone.*
● *Check prevailing weather conditions.*
● *Find out about the river in advance, both where you can put in and how difficult the paddling will be.*
● *Learn first aid and resuscitation techniques.*

RIGHT

During a course, all the equipment is provided.

T here is an element of risk in canoeing. Safety techniques will be covered on your first course. It is essential that you are a confident swimmer. Even if you don't take up white-water kayaking you may find yourself capsized accidentally on flat

Hazards to avoid on rivers
● *Overhanging trees on the outside of bends and submerged trees in the main flow.*
● *Weirs and low head dams.*
● *Moored craft.*
● *Anglers and other river users.*

water and need to swim to the shore with your kayak.

The capsize drill involves getting out of an upturned kayak and swimming with it to the shore. This is particularly tricky when wearing a spraydeck on a closed-in cockpit. Learning how to perform rescues quickly will save a lot of time and energy when you do capsize.

If there are other canoeists nearby you might not have to swim to the shore. The ultimate form of self-rescue is the roll, a technique developed by the Inuit in Greenland to prevent them having to swim in the

ABOVE

Rescue practice is essential.

ABOVE

A novice paddler receives useful tips from an instructor during white-water training.

icy Arctic waters. This involves righting the kayak after it has overturned, without getting out and is best learnt in a swimming pool. Rolling really comes into its own when you are kayaking on white water or in surf and the ability to right yourself within seconds is preferable to a long swim.

The way to improve your canoeing is to practise. Books on technique will help you to understand the finer points of paddle strokes and manoeuvres, but they are not a substitute for the real thing. The more you paddle, the fitter you will get and the more confident you will be in your own ability. Where you go from your first lessons is up to you. With two-thirds of the world's surface covered in water, the possibilities are endless.

Over the top

Jesse Sharp of Ocoee, Tennessee, became one of the many daredevils to attempt the Niagara Falls, although his attempt was the first in a kayak. Confident of his success, he made dinner reservations for the celebration. The power of the Falls proved too much. Jesse's kayak was recovered near the base of the Falls, but he hadn't survived.

EQUIPMENT

Canoeing's roots are in the kayaks of the Inuit and the canoes of the Native Americans. In fact, in Britain we often use the wrong words for our boats. A boat with a covered deck and a cockpit should really be called a kayak, but is often called a canoe. And an open boat is really a canoe, but is often known as a Canadian. In this book, covered boats are called kayaks and open boats are called canoes.

Visit any canoe club or specialist shop and you will soon realize how different the designs are, and start wondering what type of kayak you really need. You will need a specialist kayak if you want to take part in slalom, racing or sea kayaking, but for most activities a general-purpose kayak is adequate.

General-purpose kayaks: the manoeuvrability of a kayak is dependent on its rocker. This is the amount of curve in the bottom of the boat from bow to stern. A kayak with no rocker is easy to paddle in a straight line. One with a lot of rocker is easy to turn, but more difficult to keep in a straight line. General-purpose kayaks are a compromise between the two. They are good at going in a straight line, and not too hard to turn.

RIGHT

The Inuit kayaks of Greenland were the forerunners of modern kayaks.

12

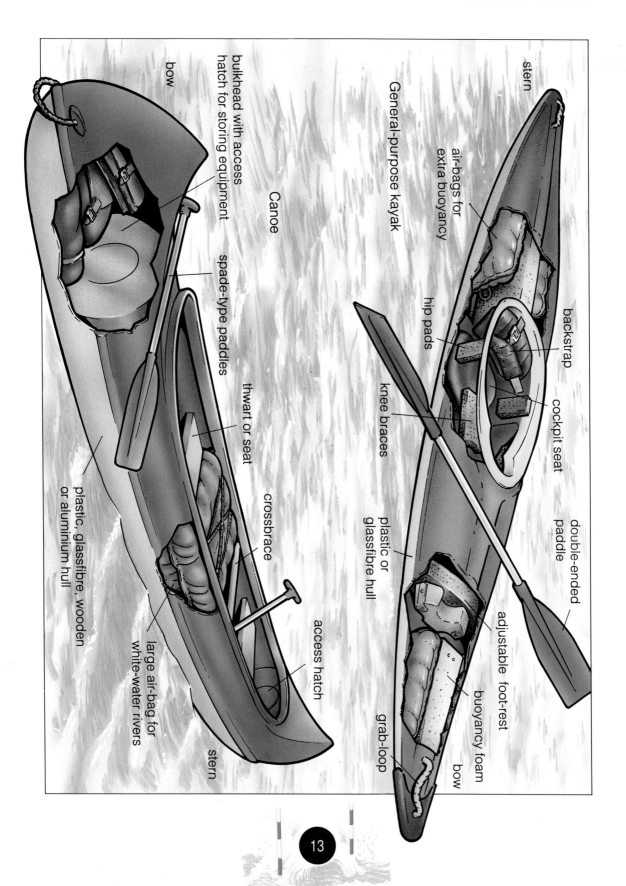

General-purpose kayak

stern

air-bags for
extra buoyancy

hip pads

knee braces

backstrap

cockpit seat

double-ended
paddle

plastic or
glassfibre hull

adjustable foot-rest

buoyancy foam

bow

grab-loop

Canoe

bow

bulkhead with access
hatch for storing equipment

spade-type paddles

thwart or seat

crossbrace

access hatch

large air-bag for
white-water rivers

plastic, glassfibre, wooden
or aluminium hull

stern

There are many different makes and styles to choose from, so it is best to try out as many as you can before deciding which one you really prefer. Cost will be an important factor. Cheaper kayaks are made from glassfibre and resin, and the more expensive ones are made in plastic. Plastic is less likely to break and virtually maintenance-free. The popularity of plastic kayaks in recent years has encouraged healthy competition amongst manufacturers and prices are now quite reasonable.

Any kayak you choose should have a certain number of safety features. These include adjustable foot-rests, strong grab-loops at either end and enough internal buoyancy to keep the kayak afloat when waterlogged.

Touring kayaks are longer than general-purpose kayaks and have less rocker, for paddling in a straight line. Touring kayaks come in one- or two-person versions and are ideal for day trips or long-distance tours on rivers, canals and lakes. With a spraydeck fitted, touring kayaks can tackle easy white water, and there is usually enough space to store camping equipment and supplies for overnight trips. Some touring kayaks have larger, open cockpits.

The general-purpose kayak is suitable for most white-water rivers, but as white-water kayaking has grown over recent years there have been radical changes in the kayaks used. Some are designed for long wilderness trips and others developed specially for narrow and technical mountain rivers.

White-water kayaks are often classified by their volume (the amount of space taken up by a kayak) and their length. High-volume kayaks provide greater stability in white water and are often used on expeditions, because they also provide more storage space.

General-purpose kayaks fall into the medium volume category and are excellent to learn in and will cater for most of your kayaking adventures. Low-volume kayaks are usually those designed for competitive slalom or playboating.

The length of the kayak affects its ability to turn, and on mountain rivers which are often narrow and steep, being able to turn quickly is essential.

For mountain rivers a range of short kayaks has been developed, with rounded ends to avoid snagging on rocks, but with almost the same volume as a general-purpose kayak.

The other items that you need to complete your kayaking kit are a paddle, buoyancy aid, spraydeck and helmet.

Like kayaks, paddles come in a wide variety of styles and constructions. Kayak paddles have blades on each end of the shaft set at ninety degrees to each other. This is called feathering. It helps the upper blade to slice more easily through the air while the lower one is being pulled back through the water. Choose the correct length of paddle by standing it upright and reaching up to the top blade. If you can just curl your fingers over the top of the blade, then the paddle is the right length for you.

Paddles can be simple plywood blades on an aluminium shaft, hand-crafted all-wooden paddles, or hi-tech composite fibreglass, resin and aluminium constructions designed for the roughest use. Most blades are curved because this gives them more support in the water.

ABOVE

The right equipment is essential if you are to kayak safely.

The Mike Jones Rally, which attracts around 2,000 paddlers annually, holds one of the more bizarre races in canoeing, The Cardboard Canoe Race. Strict rules allow no serious entries. Fancy dress and theme boats are the order of the day and canoes must be constructed only from cardboard and sticky tape. Many of the entries sink or capsize before they reach the finish line.

The buoyancy aid is the most important item of equipment you will buy. It is designed to keep you afloat and protect you from rocks if you are white-water or surf kayaking. The shape of the buoyancy aid allows your arms free movement. Choose one that fits tightly without being uncomfortable. Buoyancy aids for expedition or white-water paddling often have extra buoyancy to keep your head well out of the water. They may also feature pockets for storing equipment, such as flares and a survival kit, and a built-in safety harness for rescue situations.

Spraydecks are necessary to keep water out of the kayak. Even on flat water they keep drips and splashes off your legs. Spraydecks are made from nylon or neoprene and they should feature a strong release loop, so that they can be pulled off the cockpit quickly and easily in an emergency.

Helmets are useful when learning to canoe, to stop you from being

BELOW

Canoe trips don't have to be all white water and waterfalls.

bashed on the head by someone else's paddle. They are essential when paddling on shallow rocky rivers and white water where you could hit a rock below the surface if you have capsized. Your helmet should be a good fit and comfortable. Make sure that it gives good protection to your forehead.

The choice of equipment can be bewildering, but you will soon find out what suits you best. If you have any doubts, ask around and see what other people are using. Once you have your own equipment you will be free to plan your own river adventures.

ABOVE

Two kayakers wearing buoyancy aids, helmets and cagoules.

RIGHT

Room for two! The front storage compartment of this kayak has many uses.

RIVER ADVENTURE

At breakfast we studied the maps, checking the topography of the surrounding country, looking for roads or tracks that would take us further upstream to begin our day's kayaking.

'How far?' someone asked.

'It's about forty kilometres with only a few small rapids,' I replied.

All we had to do was to get there. Although it was only fifty kilometres, the drive to our put-in point would take a couple of hours. There were few roads, only dirt tracks and the added hazard of wild animals. This wasn't a safari park but the African bush on the banks of the Zambezi River.

After two hours, cramped in an old Land Rover with seven kayaks strapped on the roof, we finally reached the put-in point. The day's

ABOVE

Elephants eyeing the passing canoeists.

LEFT

Approaching elephants on the Upper Zambezi River.

journey would take between four and seven hours, depending on the speed of the river and how fast we paddled. There was no need to rush.

A wide expanse of water lay ahead of us. On either side were palm-fringed, sandy banks. Baboons skipped from branch to branch in the trees, one moment still and watchful, the next screeching and crashing through the undergrowth. Waterbuck and impala, drinking at the river's edge, sensed our intrusion and sprang away into the trees. Only the great kudu antelope stood firm, eyeing us suspiciously.

As we rounded a bend in the river we were faced with three large elephants standing in the shallow waters. Cautiously we edged away from them, not wanting to be on the receiving end of their feet!

There were a few small rapids in this section of river but all were very easy to navigate, with straight runs along well-defined channels. The only hazards were the hippos and crocodiles that lived in the river.

Every so often we banged on the decks of the kayaks. The hippos, grazing on the river-bed, would rise to the surface ahead of us, giving us enough time to avoid them.

Crocodiles are different. They often float with only their snouts on the surface of the water, and are difficult to spot. They lurk in the still pools, and for every one we saw we knew that there were others just below the water's surface.

As we neared the end of the day's paddle we began to pass small villages. Dug-out canoes lay idle on the banks, a stark contrast to our hi-tech polyethylene kayaks.

BELOW

Surfing the 'Thunder Waves' on the Zambezi River.

RIGHT

A novel way to
transport a kayak
in Kathmandu in
Nepal.

O ur trip down the Zambezi River was a very special adventure, and the sense of excitement on that day was little different to my first explorations of the rivers and canals around my home, and weekend trips with the youth group.

Day trips are the easiest trips to

organize, and can be anywhere from a few to forty or more kilometres, depending on water conditions. In slow-moving canals or rivers you may travel at a rate of only three kilometres an hour. On a river that is flowing more quickly you may double your speed. Speed is not really that important. Take time to explore the side streams, creeks and backwaters that you come across, and keep an eye out for wildlife. Imagine that you are in the heart of Africa surrounded by crocodiles. . .

On any trip there are some essential precautions that you must take. These will be covered in your first kayaking course but the most important points are:

● Plan your route and tell someone where you are going.

● Always have a minimum of three people in your group.

● Wear appropriate clothing for the weather conditions and carry spare warm clothes.

● Take a packed lunch, drink and spare food.

● Get an experienced person to go with you.

BELOW

Kayakers pack their boats before a descent of the Modi Khola River in Nepal.

You should be quite experienced before you plan your own adventure with friends. Multi-day trips or touring require detailed preparation because you need to carry all your camping gear, drink and food. It is best to gain experience by starting with a single overnight stop.

Equipment should be stowed so it doesn't unbalance the boat, so don't put all the heavy items in the back! Equally important is ensuring that food and clothing is packed in watertight bags or containers. Many people cut down on weight by using bivouac bags instead of tents and by carrying dehydrated (dried out) food. After a few trips you will soon find out what equipment suits you best.

ABOVE

Exploring a river near your home can be a real adventure.

RIGHT

Multi-day trips should be prepared carefully.

SEA KAYAKING

The roar of breaking waves, crashing line upon line towards the shore, is enough to send a surfer into a frenzy trying to get out there. On holiday weekends the sea is packed with swimmers and surfers, all occupying a small area close to the shore. Beyond them, there is nothing but a clear blue ocean stretching to the horizon, disappearing out of sight around the headlands on either side. This is the territory of the sea kayaker, away from the crowds, exploring rocky coastlines and secluded beaches where the only access is from the sea, paddling beneath natural arches eroded by the force of the sea and skimming quietly into dark caves.

The sea provides kayakers and canoeists with an endless range of possibilities. You can go on short, coastal day trips, visit nearby islands or undertake lengthy sea voyages.

A general-purpose kayak is suitable for a day trip, but you need a specialist sea kayak for longer journeys. Sea kayaks are very similar to the kayaks used by Greenland Inuit. They are long and narrow, designed to cut through waves and cover long distances. The bow and stern are sealed up, and there are watertight hatches on the deck. This makes the kayak virtually unsinkable and provides dry storage areas for equipment. Deck lines hold equipment the paddler might need

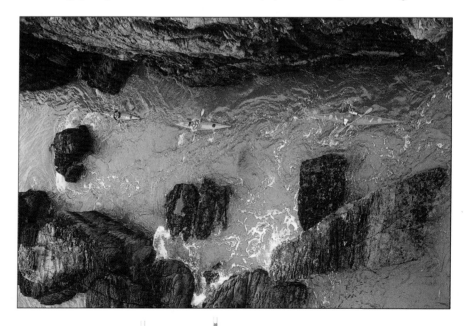

ABOVE

The thrill of surfing on a highly manoeuvrable wave ski.

LEFT

A group of sea kayakers pass between cliffs and stacks. Note the long, thin shape of the sea kayak and the deck hatches fore and aft.

quickly, such as spare paddles, maps and fishing tackle.

Having the right kayak is only part of a successful adventure. Sea kayaking demands a knowledge of weather patterns and tidal streams, and good navigation. At sea the weather can change suddenly, leaving you out on the ocean in dangerous conditions.

There is another kind of sea kayaking, for which you only need a general-purpose kayak and a good wave: surfing. Like stand-up surfboards, kayaks catch the waves and ride in on them. If the waves break you have two options: you can do a loop or go for a bongo slide.

Loops are done by slowing down as the wave breaks; the wave will then pick up the back of the boat, the front will drive down and the boat will go end over end. Bongo sliding is bracing sideways on the wave as it carries you in (while doing this you should keep an eye out for anyone in your way). If a collision is likely then go for a roll and the wave will pass you by.

Surf kayaking also has a competitive side. This has led to the development of surf shoes (flat-bottomed surf kayaks) and wave skis, which are similar to a surfboard, except that you sit on them and use paddles. They are as manoeuvrable as surfboards but pick up the waves a lot earlier.

WHITE WATER

After a week of preparation on the Alpine rivers near Innsbruck, we drove through Italy into Austria to attempt the River Isel. The guide book gave the river a grade 5 rating so we knew that we would be in for some hard kayaking.

As the road climbed up the valley we could see the river below. At each bend there were stretches of white water lasting several hundred metres, and we could see how the river had earned its reputation. At river level the sight was breathtaking – the thundering water, crashing through a jumble of giant boulders, would give us few places to stop. Everyone was nervous as we inspected possible routes down the first major rapid. After ten minutes of discussion, we scrambled back to our kayaks.

With spraydecks on, helmets buckled and buoyancy aids secured we pushed off. The speed of the water was exhilarating and the hundred metres to the first breakout passed in seconds. The main hazard, a large fall, was next.

LEFT

A kayaker heads into a tricky rapid.

RIGHT

Coming out of a large drop – the force of the water on the back deck almost stands the kayak on end.

River gradings

White-water rivers are graded according to their difficulty. Grades given in river guides are usually for favourable conditions; they may change depending on river levels or recent rock slides and fallen trees.

Grade 1: Easy. Moving water with occasional small rapids; few or no obstacles.

Grade 2: Medium. Small rapids but easy to navigate with regular waves.

Grade 3: Difficult. Rapids with irregular waves and hazards that need to be avoided. Complex manoeuvring often required and inspection may be needed.

Grade 4: Very difficult. Large rapids and falls, precise manoeuvring required; dangerous hazards. Inspection necessary and rescue difficult. Rolling ability often needed.

Grade 5: Extremely difficult. Complex and difficult rapids with dangerous hydraulics and difficult route-finding. Inspection essential. Rolling ability essential. Rescue difficult or impossible. Hazard to life.

Grade 6: Limit of navigation. Grade 5 carried to the extreme of navigation; nearly impossible. A fine line between success or failure. It is better to spectate!

ABOVE

When negotiating a narrow fall, care is needed to avoid hitting the rocks.

There was little time for preparation, but I was still on the correct line. I paddled hard into the drop, putting all my strength into a strong brace to punch through the stopper. The water crashed all around and I pulled hard on the paddle. Daylight again. . . I was through. But there was no time to relax as more rapids lay ahead! I glanced back quickly to see Richard pulling through the fall and Guy following close behind him. We were safe.

G rade 5 white water like the section on the River Isel is only possible when you have gained sufficient skills and have built up your experience of white water on lower grade rivers. Not everyone enjoys this type of white water. Many people prefer longer, easier rapids on which mistakes are unlikely to be life-threatening.

Rapids are usually tackled in sections. The slack water behind rocks is used for a rest. These areas of slack water are known as eddies, and kayakers will break out of the fast water into them to stop and survey the route downstream, before breaking back into the rapid. This is called eddy hopping.

If you're not sure what's downstream, you will have to head for the bank and get out to inspect the river. A thin horizon line ahead may signal a waterfall. Waterfalls are treated with caution as there may be dangers in the pools below.

RIGHT

Extreme waterfall running on the River Rizzanese in Corsica.

29

COMPETITION

Competition requires a certain level of determination and fitness to succeed. Skill and experience are also important, and the equipment used has been developed to achieve the best possible performance.

You don't have to be of world championship standard to enjoy competitions. All competitive kayaking events are fun to enter, and levels of competition have been graded to enable people of all ages and abilities to take part.

Competitions attract large numbers of both spectators and

RIGHT

In slalom racing, the competitors must negotiate a number of gates on a winding course.

LEFT

The look of concentration is evident on this slalom canoeist's face as he heads towards the next gate.

competitors, and a weekend's slalom or racing event inevitably turns into a large social gathering. Anyone can make new friends, with a similar enthusiasm for the sport.

S lalom canoeing is regarded as the ultimate test of kayak control, fitness and ability to read the water. The competitor is timed over a short stretch of white water, through a course of numbered gates. A slalom gate consists of two suspended poles. Green and white poles indicate that the competitor must pass through the gate going downstream, and red and white indicate that it must be taken going upstream. If any part of her or

ABOVE

Richard Fox, one of the greatest slalom canoeists of all time.

his paddles, boat or body touches the poles, time penalties are added to the time of the competitor. The paddler with the fastest overall time out of two runs over the white-water course wins the competition.

The slalom kayak has developed over the years; the early designs were similar to today's high-volume kayaks but now they are low volume with almost flat decks to enable the kayak to slide under the poles.

Entering a slalom event will not

Richard Fox

Richard Fox had already won the World Slalom Championships three times; at the 1987 World Championships event at Bourg, France, the question on everyone's lips was whether Fox could hold his title an unprecedented fourth time. Fox's first run of the competition was to be the fastest of the whole World Championships, but a penalty on gate 13 pushed him into second place. On his second run, he also produced a fast time, but again was unlucky at gate 13 when the tip of his kayak touched a pole. Fox was relegated to fourth place behind the new world champion, Anton Prijon of Germany. Many thought that Fox's long reign had come to an end, but in the 1989 World Championships on the Savage River in the USA he took them by surprise. Although his second run began with a penalty on gate 1 he moved into overdrive, taking 2.47 seconds off his previous run, enough to give him a substantial lead for his fourth World Championships win. Fox proved that he is perhaps the greatest slalom paddler of all time.

only give you your first taste of the sport, but also help to improve your paddling skills.

Wild-water racing is tough and demanding, not only physically but also mentally. Much of the race is spent alone, without other competitors or spectators nearby. A wild-water race is held over three kilometres of a river with at least grade 3 rapids. The ability to read the water and assess hazards quickly in order to choose the safest and fastest route makes a lot of difference to the overall time. A bad route, a rock hit or a capsize will lose vital seconds.

The wild-water racing kayak is

RIGHT

A river racing double kayak plunges into a fall during a competition.

designed for maximum forward speed through rapids. The long, flat keel and V-shaped bottom cut through the waves, and the high volume helps to lift it out of the water. The wing-like section behind the seat provides extra buoyancy and stability when turning.

Competitors start at a minimum of thirty second intervals, with a five second countdown to the start. From then on every stroke must count. If the person behind you catches you, you must give way. Otherwise you could be disqualified for obstruction.

The word 'marathon' makes people think of the 42.2 kilometre running event. Kayak marathons are fortunately much shorter, with races between five and seven kilometres long in the lower divisions and twenty or more in the top divisions. Marathon racing in kayaks involves getting past obstacles such as locks, weirs and rapids. Some of these require portaging (carrying the kayak around the obstacle).

Most marathons have a mass start

BELOW

Marathon paddlers portaging their kayak during a race.

ABOVE

Canoe competition, Chinese style. This Dragon Boat race in Beijing, China, is a popular sprint-racing event.

The 200-kilometre Devizes to Westminster Race is one of the toughest non-stop races in the world. Winning times are under sixteen hours, but many competitors aim to complete the race within twenty-four hours.

The Arctic Canoe Race starts over 400 kilometres north of the Arctic Circle at Kilpisjarvi, Finland, close to the point where the borders of Sweden, Norway, and Finland meet. The race covers 537 kilometres and lasts for about six days.

rather like a grand prix motor racing event. The person who gets to the front of the pack has the advantage at the first portage.

Races are held at national and club level. Many local clubs organize their own mini-marathon series. In club races specialist boats are not essential and the emphasis is on taking part rather than winning. These events are a good way to get fitter, as you try to improve your best time over a set course. Specialist marathon kayaks are long and narrow and feel

Molokai Hoe canoe race

The Molokai Hoe outrigger canoe race is run between the Hawaiian islands of Oahu and Molokai, a distance of sixty-four kilometres. The race has been held every year since 1952 and commemorates the invasion of Oahu in 1795 by the Hawaiian chief Kamahameka who, after crossing the Kaiwi Channel with a fleet of war canoes, defeated the rival warriors. The outrigger canoes are up to fourteen metres long. Three of the six paddlers are replaced every fifteen minutes by fresh ones, who board the boat from the water as it passes.

ABOVE

Paddling an outrigger canoe in Hawaii.

very unstable when you first sit in them. Like bicycles, they feel more stable once you are on the move. Marathon kayaks are steered with a foot-operated rudder so that maximum forward paddling power can be maintained at all times.

Sprint-racing is comparable to track athletics. Racers line up at the start and race on flat water. The distances for international and Olympic events are 500 and 1,000 metres. The annual world championship event also includes a 10,000-metre long-distance race, which is hardly a sprint!

Another popular sprint-racing event is Dragon Boat racing. These spectacular races involve canoes of up to twelve metres in length crewed by a team of twenty paddlers. The paddling stroke is maintained to the rhythm of a drummer in the boat.

Canoe polo is a great way to test your reactions. Two teams of five kayakers try to score goals using a football. The goals are suspended two metres above the water at either end and the ball can be passed by throwing or by flicking it with the paddle. Once you've got the ball you can only hold on to it for five seconds before it has to be passed. Dangerous use of the paddle, obstruction, barging, or the ball going out of play gives possession to the other team. Capsizing your opponent is allowed, but only if the ball is in her or his possession. Most players take a dip, and you must be able to roll if you want to get back into the game quickly.

While you can set your own game up using general-purpose kayaks, specialist polo kayaks are short with rounded ends. Paddle blades must not have sharp edges and a face guard is often worn for extra protection.

BELOW

Going for goal during a canoe polo match.

PLAYBOATING

Playboating, hotdogging, rodeo. All the names mean the same thing: freestyle kayaking for fun. Playboating is full of action, skill and extreme manoeuvres requiring a high degree of skill.

To play, all you need is a nice friendly stopper or a large wave on which to perform acrobatics in a kayak. Loops, popouts, skyrockets and pirouettes are the basis of many stunts and the essence is to perform them with style. Playboaters have perfected numerous tricks with their paddles, twirling them above their heads and throwing them into the air while still balancing on the wave. The latest fashion is performing stunts without using a paddle: a true test of skill. The real experts can juggle oranges or balls while surfing on a wave, to the cheers of the spectators.

Rodeo events, which first developed in the USA, have now spread world-wide. They feature a series of heats comprising wave surfing, stopper riding, sprint and skills, with points awarded for style, technique and sheer bravado. If you can smile while performing these tricks you're bound to get additional bonus points.

As your white-water skills develop you will find plenty of opportunity to practise various manoeuvres, and the thrill of your first popout, as the

ABOVE

A kayaker performing a popout and paddle twirl during a rodeo competition.

LEFT

Surfing on a wave at the Rodeo World Championships.

Rodeo World Championships
The first World Rodeo Championships was held in 1990 on The Bitches, a tidal overfall off the coast of South Wales. The overall winner, and the first world champion, was Jan Kellner of Augsburg, Germany. Part of the Skills heat involved an eight metre seal launch off a cliff, those who refused incurred extra penalty points!

front of the kayak dives down and you stand it vertically on end, will set your pulse racing. The techniques used in playboating become important when running extreme white-water rivers. Being confident in a stopper and knowing how to get out will boost your confidence on white water.

T he most extreme playboat is known as a squirtboat. These are very low-volume kayaks that are built to suit the weight of the paddler so that they float just on the surface of the water. The very flat and thin bow and stern enable very complex and radical moves to be undertaken. The most bizarre of all these moves is known as the mystery move. Squirtboaters can paddle into a jet of water and submerge the whole kayak underwater, only to reappear skyrocketing upwards several metres downstream. What happens below the surface is a mystery known only to the squirtboater.

Squirtboat moves have such names as blasting, rocksplats, meltdowns, black attacks and cartwheels. Learning each move can take hours. Squirtboats are almost as much fun to watch as to paddle.

EXPEDITIONS

O n our arrival in Lima, the capital of Peru, we had hired a small bus to take our kayaks and equipment on the journey southwards along the Pan American Highway. We were forced to squeeze the kayaks into the bus, which had no roof-rack, leaving little room for anyone to sit. After twenty-four cramped hours of non-stop driving we arrived in the small village of Haumbo, in the coastal mountains of southern Peru.

Four months of planning had got us this far. Flights and sponsorship had been obtained, and food and equipment lists had been drawn up to make sure we were properly equipped. The only thing left was to get to the river.

There were no roads into the depths of what is regarded as the world's deepest canyon, only a rough mule track skirting precipitous gorges. Armed with a phrase book of Latin-American Spanish we entered the only shop in the village. 'Donde puedo encontrar tres burros por favor?' The shop owner understood our request for three mules to transport our kayaks into the canyon!

We were not the first kayakers to attempt the Colca Canyon. Previous expeditions had left the local population with a genuine concern for the life expectancy of anyone crazy enough to attempt the river. We showed them a poster of a kayaker running a ten-metre waterfall in

ABOVE

Loading the
kayaks on to
mules at the start
of the expedition.

LEFT

At Lima in Peru
our kayaks were
squeezed into a
bus, leaving little
space for any one
else!

Colca Canyon

*The Polish Canoandes
expedition were the first
explorers to tackle the Colca
Canyon in Peru. They
attempted the entire length of
the Canyon in May 1981, an
expedition that took nearly a
month to complete. The first
forty-four kilometres from
Cabanaconde to Canco took
eleven days, a section they
described as a combination of
canoeing and mountaineering.*

Corsica in an attempt to prove that
we knew what we were doing. It had
the opposite effect; now they were
sure we were crazy! The following
morning, having spent the night in
the local police station because there
were no hotels, the mules arrived
with their two owners. The kayaks
were strapped on the mules' backs
and, having said our farewells, we
trooped out of town into the depths of
the Colca Canyon.

The eight-hour walk in was long and hot. In many places the path crossed dangerous slopes of rock fragments where one slip would have sent us sliding hundreds of metres down. We reached the river with only enough time to find firewood before darkness fell.

During the night we were woken by the rumbling thunder of falling rocks close by. We had been warned that rock falls were one of the hazards in the canyon and we wondered if we ought to sleep with our helmets on. At first light we crawled from our bivouac bags, relit the fire and began the task of packing our kayaks for the three-day journey ahead. Food, clothing and other equipment went into tough waterproof bags that were secured in the kayak. Even after cutting down our equipment to the bare minimum, we still managed to fill all the available space in the boats.

BELOW

The long walk in on precipitous canyon paths.

ABOVE

Deep in the heart of the Colca Canyon.

Mike Jones

Mike Jones inspired a whole generation of paddlers with his famous first descent of Everest's Dudh Kosi River, which set a world altitude record for canoeing at 5,330 metres on an icy lake high on the Khumbu Glacier. His other hair-raising expeditions included a descent of the Nile River in Africa and the Maipire Rapids on the Orinoco River in South America. Sadly, Mike Jones' adventures ended in 1978, when he drowned on the Braldo River, Pakistan, while rescuing a colleague.

Within a couple of hours we were ready for the off. Once we had started we knew that there would be no turning back – it was virtually impossible to walk out of the canyon until we reached the end. Even so, we were looking forward to the rapids ahead and the wild remote scenery that the canyon would offer.

We edged out into the fast-flowing water and headed into the first rapid of the day. The river descent had finally begun.

ACCESS

As your enthusiasm for kayaking grows you will start to look for new waterways to explore. The growing demand for venues in recent years has led to restrictions being imposed. Many rivers are privately owned and while laws in some countries allow freedom of access to the river for the public, others do not. In these cases permission must be obtained from the owners in advance. The national body for kayaking may have an access agreement with the owners restricting the times at which a river may be used. Other rivers may have a permit system which regulates the number of users. Access agreements have arisen out of conflict with other river users, such as anglers, and the best type of agreement will allow all users reasonable access to pursue their sport. It is important that you find out if the river you intend to use has such an agreement in force. Ignoring it will give kayakers a bad name and may lead to a complete ban on kayaking.

On smaller mountain rivers there is little room for large groups and numbers should be kept small, even if it means splitting the group up and starting at different times.

Small things such as being too

Health precautions

Natural waterways, while appearing clean, contain many micro-organisms. The risk of contracting illness is small, including the much publicized Weil's disease (Leptospirosis). You should however take some sensible precautions, such as covering cuts, before exposure to water, not swallowing water and washing in clean water afterwards.

Blue-green algae, although naturally present in many waters, under certain conditions produce a 'bloom', particularly along the edge of reservoirs after long periods of hot weather. The algae can be toxic, so avoid contact. Should any accidental contact occur, wash the algae from the skin as soon as possible.

Should you become ill within two weeks of exposure to canal, river or reservoir water let your doctor know that you have been in contact with untreated water, especially if you have swallowed any. This should be done immediately so that a blood test can be carried out.

A kayaker's code of conduct

● Learn to paddle safely and avoid being a hazard or disturbance to other river users.
● Make sure your craft is safe and that sufficient safety equipment is carried at all times.
● Obey rules of navigation and any local by-laws.
● Observe access agreements where they exist or seek permission before kayaking down a river.
● Where possible use only recognized landing and launching points.
● Do not trespass on private banks or moorings.
● Avoid areas important for wintering wildfowl, nesting birds and spawning fish in the appropriate season.
● Avoid damaging banks and shoreline vegetation.
● Do everything possible to avoid pollution. Do not throw litter or rubbish into the water or leave it lying about.
● Encourage others to conserve and care for the environment and support schemes to conserve the environment.
● Remember that a paddler should take nothing but photographs and leave nothing but footprints.

noisy can offend local people. Care should be taken at all times to avoid disrupting other people's lives.

Canoeing causes no damage to the environment. There is no noisy motor or pollution, so kayaks and canoes are ideal for exploring wilderness areas and observing wildlife at close quarters. The shallow draught of the boat ensures that life below the surface of the river lies undisturbed. Even events such as slalom, river racing or long-distance competitions do not damage sensitive environments.

Glossary

Access agreement An agreement between paddlers, river owners and anglers concerning time-sharing of certain stretches of river. All access agreements should be observed.

Bivouac bag A sack made of either plastic or waterproof nylon, which protects you from wind and rain when sleeping out in the open.

Break out Manoeuvre the kayak out of the main flow of water into slack water.

Breakout Resting place, often an eddy.

Buoyancy Foam blocks or airbags; fixed in a kayak to provide flotation in the event of a capsize.

Buoyancy aid A flotation jacket designed to keep you afloat and give body protection. Not to be confused with a life jacket, which is designed to keep you face upwards should you lose consciousness.

Canoe A craft where the paddler kneels down and uses a single-bladed paddle.

Capsize Turning upside down and bailing out. Remember to hang on to your kayak.

Cockpit Compartment where the paddler sits.

Current Strong flow of water in a particular direction, not necessarily downstream.

Eddy Slack water or upstream current, usually behind an obstacle in the river.

Fall An abrupt drop in river gradient, where one is unable to see the bottom of the fall when viewed from upstream. Falls may occur in rapids.

Helmet Kayaking crash helmet to be used on rocky or rapid rivers. Must provide adequate head protection.

Kayak A boat where the paddler sits down and paddles with a two-bladed paddle.

Loop When a kayak cartwheels over after an ender or popout.

Outrigger A float on the end of a beam extending from the side of a canoe.

Portage Landing before a hazard, fall or weir and carrying your boat around it to put in below.

Popout An airborne kayak after standing it on end in the vertical position.

Rapid Fast-moving, rough water. Occurs when there is a drop in the gradient of the river or where the river flows over obstacles.

Roll Righting oneself without leaving the boat after a capsize.

Seal launch A method of entering the water from dry land while in your boat.

Slack water An area of still water.

Slalom Racing through a series of gates on rough water.

Standing wave A static wave, or hydraulic jump caused by underwater obstacles or as the river flow meets slow or slack water.

Stopper A recirculating wave caused by water flowing over an obstacle on the river bed.

Trespass Disturbing someone's property, against his or her will.

Topography   Geographic features of an area as shown on a map.

Washed-out   When a rapid is smoothed out due to high water flows.

White-water   Any water where the turbulence creates foam, giving the water a white appearance.

Further information

Australian Canoe Federation
Room 510
Sports House
157 Gloucester Street
Sydney
NEW SOUTH WALES 2000

British Canoe Union
Adbolton Lane
West Bridgford
NOTTINGHAM NG2 5AS

Canadian Canoe Association
1600 Prom. James Naismith Drive
Gloucester
ONTARIO K1B 5N4

New Zealand Canoeing Association
PO Box 3768
WELLINGTON

Further reading

Technique:

Canoeing Handbook, British Canoe Union (1989)

Kayak, W Nealy (Menasha Ridge Press, 1986)

River Rescue, L Bechdel and S Ray (Appalachian Mountain Club, 1985)

The Squirt Book, J Snyder (Menasha Ridge Press, 1987)

The White Water River Book, R Watters (Pacific Search Press, 1989)

White Water Kayaking, Ray Rowe (Salamander, 1988)

White Water Safety, Stuart Hardy (Stuart Hardy Publications, 1990)

Adventure:

Canoeing Down Everest, M Jones (Hodder and Sloughton, 1979)

Deliverance, J Dickey (Hamish Hamilton, 1970)

Does the Wet Suit You?, W Deschner (Eddie Tern Press, 1981)

Raging Rivers, Stormy Seas, T Storry (Oxford Illustrated Press, 1989)

River guides and videos:

There are river guides to most parts of the world. A list of guides can be obtained from your national organization or local canoeing shop. There are also many videos available that you may be able to hire from your local canoeing shop. These cover techniques and expeditions.

Index

(Numbers in **bold** refer to pictures as well as text.)